PHOTOGRAPHIC MEMORIES OF BRITAIN

SOUTH-EAST LONDON

Hazelle Jackson is a writer and historian specialising in local and garden history. Her family have lived in South-East London, on the Kent-Surrey border, for over four hundred years.

PHOTOGRAPHIC MEMORIES
OF BRITAIN

PHOTOGRAPHIC MEMORIES OF BRITAIN

SOUTH-EAST LONDON

HAZELLE JACKSON

First published in the United Kingdom in 2003 by
Frith Book Company Ltd

Hardback Edition 2003
ISBN 1-85937-761-0

British Library Cataloguing in Publication Data

Photographic Memories of Britain - South-East London
Hazelle Jackson

Frith Book Company Ltd
Frith's Barn, Teffont,
Salisbury, Wiltshire SP3 5QP
Tel: +44 (0) 1722 716 376
Email: info@francisfrith.co.uk
www.francisfrith.co.uk

Printed and bound in Great Britain

Front Cover: **BEXLEYHEATH,** *The Clock Tower c1950* B650022
Frontispiece: **FOREST HILL,** *London Road c1950* F179001

*The colour-tinting is for illustrative purposes only, and is not intended to be
historically accurate*

AS WITH ANY HISTORICAL DATABASE THE FRITH ARCHIVE IS CONSTANTLY
BEING CORRECTED AND IMPROVED AND THE PUBLISHERS WOULD
WELCOME INFORMATION ON OMISSIONS OR INACCURACIES

CONTENTS

FRANCIS FRITH
VICTORIAN PIONEER

FRANCIS FRITH, founder of the world-famous photographic archive, was a complex and multi-talented man. A devout Quaker and a highly successful Victorian businessman, he was philosophic by nature and pioneering in outlook.

By 1855 he had already established a wholesale grocery business in Liverpool, and sold it for the astonishing sum of £200,000, which is the equivalent today of over £15,000,000. Now a very rich man, he was able to indulge his passion for travel. As a child he had pored over travel books written by early explorers, and his fancy and imagination had been stirred by family holidays to the sublime mountain regions of Wales and Scotland. 'What lands of spirit-stirring and enriching scenes and places!' he had written. He was to return to these scenes of grandeur in later years to 'recapture the thousands of vivid and tender memories', but with a different purpose. Now in his thirties, and captivated by the new science of photography, Frith set out on a series of pioneering journeys up the Nile and to the Near East that occupied him from 1856 until 1860.

INTRIGUE AND EXPLORATION

These far-flung journeys were packed with intrigue and adventure. In his life story, written when he was sixty-three, Frith tells of being held captive by bandits, and of fighting 'an awful midnight battle to the very point of surrender with a deadly pack of hungry, wild dogs'. Wearing flowing Arab costume, Frith arrived at Akaba by camel seventy years before Lawrence of Arabia, where he encountered 'desert princes and rival sheikhs, blazing with jewel-hilted swords'.

He was the first photographer to venture beyond the sixth cataract of the Nile. Africa was still the mysterious 'Dark Continent', and Stanley and Livingstone's historic meeting was a decade into the future. The conditions for picture taking confound belief. He laboured for hours in his wicker dark-room in the sweltering heat of the desert, while the volatile chemicals fizzed dangerously in their trays. Back in London he exhibited his photographs and was 'rapturously cheered' by members of the Royal Society. His reputation as a photographer was made overnight.

VENTURE OF A LIFE-TIME

Characteristically, Frith quickly spotted the opportunity to create a new business as a specialist publisher of photographs. He lived in an era of immense and sometimes violent change.

For the poor in the early part of Victoria's reign work was exhausting and the hours long, and people had precious little free time to enjoy themselves. Most had no transport other than a cart or gig at their disposal, and rarely travelled far beyond the boundaries of their own town or village. However, by the 1870s the railways had threaded their way across the country, and Bank Holidays and half-day Saturdays had been made obligatory by Act of Parliament. All of a sudden the working man and his family were able to enjoy days out and see a little more of the world.

With typical business acumen, Francis Frith foresaw that these new tourists would enjoy having souvenirs to commemorate their days out. In 1860 he married Mary Ann Rosling and set out on a new career: his aim was to photograph every city, town and village in Britain. For the next thirty years he travelled the country by train and by pony and trap, producing fine photographs of seaside resorts and beauty spots that were keenly bought by millions of Victorians. These prints were painstakingly pasted into family albums and pored over during the dark nights of winter, rekindling precious memories of summer excursions.

THE RISE OF FRITH & CO

Frith's studio was soon supplying retail shops all over the country. To meet the demand he gathered about him a small team of photographers, and published the work of independent artist-photographers of the calibre of Roger Fenton and Francis Bedford. In order to gain some understanding of the scale of Frith's business one only has to look at the catalogue issued by Frith & Co in 1886: it runs to some 670 pages, listing not only many thousands of views of the British Isles but also many photographs of most European countries, and China, Japan, the USA and Canada - note the sample page shown on page 9 from the hand-written Frith & Co ledgers recording the pictures. By 1890 Frith had created the greatest specialist photographic publishing company in the world, with over 2,000 sales outlets - more than the combined number that Boots and WH Smith have today! The picture on the next page shows the Frith & Co display board at Ingleton in the Yorkshire Dales (left of window). Beautifully constructed with a mahogany frame and gilt inserts, it could display up to a dozen local scenes.

POSTCARD BONANZA

The ever-popular holiday postcard we know today took many years to develop. In 1870 the Post Office issued the first plain cards, with a pre-printed stamp on one face. In 1894 they allowed other publishers' cards to be sent through the mail with an attached adhesive halfpenny stamp. Demand grew rapidly, and in 1895 a new size of postcard was permitted called the court card, but there was little room for illustration. In 1899, a year after Frith's death, a new card measuring 5.5 x 3.5 inches became the standard format, but it was not until 1902 that the divided back came into being, so that the address and message could be on one face and a full-size illustration on the other. Frith & Co were in the vanguard of postcard development: Frith's sons Eustace and Cyril continued their father's monumental task, expanding the number of views offered to the public and recording more and more places in Britain, as the coasts and countryside were opened up to mass travel.

Francis Frith had died in 1898 at his villa in Cannes, his great project still growing. The archive he created continued in business for another seventy years. By 1970 it contained over a third of a million pictures showing 7,000 British towns and villages.

FRANCIS FRITH'S LEGACY

Frith's legacy to us today is of immense significance and value, for the magnificent archive of evocative photographs he created provides a unique record of change in the cities, towns and villages throughout Britain over a century and more. Frith and his fellow studio photographers revisited locations many times down the years to update their views, compiling for us an enthralling and colourful pageant of British life and character.

We are fortunate that Frith was dedicated to recording the minutiae of everyday life. For it is this sheer wealth of visual data, the painstaking chronicle of changes in dress, transport, street layouts, buildings, housing, engineering and landscape that captivates us so much today. His remarkable images offer us a powerful link with the past and with the lives of our ancestors.

THE VALUE OF THE ARCHIVE TODAY

Computers have now made it possible for Frith's many thousands of images to be accessed almost instantly. Frith's images are increasingly used as visual resources, by social historians, by researchers into genealogy and ancestry, by architects and town planners, and by teachers involved in local history projects.

In addition, the archive offers every one of us an opportunity to examine the places where we and our families have lived and worked down the years. Highly successful in Frith's own era, the archive is now, a century and more on, entering a new phase of popularity. Historians consider the Francis Frith Collection to be of prime national importance. It is the only archive of its kind remaining in private ownership. Francis Frith's archive is now housed in an historic timber barn in the beautiful village of Teffont in Wiltshire. Its founder would not recognize the archive office as it is today. In place of the many thousands of dusty boxes containing glass plate negatives and an all-pervading odour of photographic chemicals, there are now ranks of computer screens. He would be amazed to watch his images travelling round the world at unimaginable speeds through internet lines.

The archive's future is both bright and exciting. Francis Frith, with his unshakeable belief in making photographs available to the greatest number of people, would undoubtedly approve of what is being done today with his lifetime's work. His photographs depicting our shared past are now bringing pleasure and enlightenment to millions around the world a century and more after his death.

SOUTH-EAST LONDON

AN INTRODUCTION

FOR over two thousand years, the south-east of England has been the first line of defence against invaders and the gateway to the rest of Britain. The expansion of London into its south-east hinterland is inextricably entwined with these factors, and with the history of northern Kent.

After the defeat of the Catuvellauni tribe in AD 43, Roman rule was established and enforced from strategic forts around the country linked by surfaced roads. Among the best known is Watling Street, which linked the capital Londinium (London) to Canterbury and the coast at Dover, where the Roman fleet, the Classicus Britannicum, was moored. Settlements soon grew up along the road, now the A2, which still runs along the old Roman route for much of its length. The Thames was the main route by water into London, and the Romans found early on that they could use the rising tides to arrive at and leave the capital.

ERITH, *The Thames c1950* E58022

During their long occupation of England, the Romans cultivated the rich agricultural hinterland of Kent to the south-east of London, building farms and market gardens to supply fruit and vegetables and even wine to the expanding capital. Wealthy Romans lived in large villas on massive estates (like the recently excavated Crofton Roman villa at Orpington).

Commerce was active and prosperous during the Roman occupation. Wool from sheep grazing on the Downs in Kent was exported across Europe. Limestone was quarried for construction in the area, which also encouraged the local manufacture of bricks. The ironstone in the clays of the Kentish weald was developed as the principal source of iron in the province, and the Weald was the location of an important iron smelting industry.

But with the slow collapse of the Roman Empire, the Romans left Kent - and Britain as a whole - during the first decade of the fifth century, settlements like Dartford declined in importance, the main Roman roads fell into disrepair, and the general standard of living was greatly reduced.

After the Romans left, London's fortunes rose and fell in the following centuries as marauding tribes of Anglo-Saxons and Vikings arrived by sea and conquered, or were defeated by, the local inhabitants. Their successes can be traced in the names of modern settlements in Kent and south-east London, which bear Anglo-Saxon names like Ceosol Hyrst (modern Chiselhurst).

By the ninth century, London's fortunes were reviving as the Saxons reoccupied the old Roman city under King Alfred. By the tenth century, London's overseas trade was growing, along with wharves and warehouses; London became an international port in a commercial network, which stretched all round the North Sea and well into the Baltic. Gradually, as the city grew, it expanded into the surrounding countryside, including south-eastwards into northern Kent.

In the Middle Ages, the Plantagent kings built themselves a pleasant palace at Eltham, whose traces can still be appreciated today.

In 1216, Dover fell under attack from Prince Louis of France, and in 1217 the French fleet was defeated off Sandwich. In 1295, French forces burned much of Dover to the ground. In the following century the French continued to attack along the Kent coast, and in 1457 they again raided Sandwich.

It was clear that defending London from the south-east was of crucial military importance, and in the 16th century Henry VII built the first royal dockyards at Deptford. The creation of these yards in Deptford and Woolwich stimulated development there. In Woolwich the building of the dockyard led to the establishment of the Royal Arsenal, and to the formation of the Royal Regiments of Artillery, and the Royal Military Academy.

The threat of attack from the east through Kent remained a very real danger following the humiliating incident in 1667 when the Dutch fleet sailed up the Medway. After this, the threat of invasion via the Thames was taken very seriously, and the defences of London from the south-east were strengthened. At Greenwich on the Thames the Stuart and Hanoverian kings laid the foundations of our maritime heritage in the 17th century.

As the British Empire grew in power and influence during the 17th and 18th centuries, so London expanded at its hub. By 1720 there were 750,000 people living in London, which was now the world's busiest port, and at the end of the century the London Docks were built to cope with the trade. Travellers rode or tramped up Watling Street (the old Roman road) as London expanded out into the surrounding countryside.

At the same time, immigrants from mainland Europe arrived and brought with them new skills and knowledge. In the 16th century, Flemish weavers settled in Kent to take advantage of that county's prosperous wool industry; they brought with them new varieties of hops and the knowledge of how to use them effectively in beer. Settlements grew up south-east of the city in places like Lewisham at the confluence of the Ravensbourne and Quaggy rivers.

With the arrival of the stagecoach, new routes sprang up, and coaching inns and livery stables were built to service the growing passenger traffic in the 18th century. Early villages like Bexleyheath developed along these roads as communities grew up to service the travellers, and communications improved. Market gardening was widespread as farms in the Kent hinterland grew fruit and vegetables for London; the chalk fields around Farnborough were famous for strawberries.

In the 18th century wealthy men and women, seeking a respite from the noise and disease of the city, built large country estates in areas like Foots Cray in Northern Kent; they were attracted by the clear air, rural countryside and plentiful water. William Pitt the Younger, the Prime Minister, had an estate at Holwood near modern-day Biggin Hill. During the 19th

century Victorian men of arts, letters and science like William Morris, Charles Dickens and Charles Darwin moved to Kent on the edge of south-east London to live and work in its leafy countryside.

The biggest change came with the arrival of the railways in the 19th century. Developers and local landowners were not slow to realise rail's potential, and London exploded dramatically out into Kent during the late 19th and early 20th centuries. Developers and speculators raced to attract commuters, workers from London, to live outside the city itself and travel on the train into town for work.

Londoners now took buses and made trips by road and river out to the countryside south-east of London to enjoy their leisure there. Some decided to settle there permanently, and the villages expanded. In recognition of the growing size of London, the London County Council was formed in 1889 from historic parts of Surrey, Kent and Middlesex. From Kent this included the former metropolitan boroughs of Deptford, Greenwich and Lewisham.

But war was approaching. The area around Woolwich expanded as factories grew up to build armaments in the build up to, and during, World War I in the early 20th century. After World War I, society underwent radical changes; the developers moved in again, and many of the old country estates to the south-east of the capital were broken up for development. Housing estates built for the new and aspiring middle classes sprang up across a wide swathe of rural farmland. The ribbon development of mock Tudor estates, now so familiar a part of south-east London, took shape.

With World War II a new and lethal form of warfare was unleashed upon London, and the residents of the south-east of the city took the brunt of the German bombs. The Royal Air Force fought and won a great victory in the skies over Biggin Hill in the Battle of Britain, but Londoners paid an appalling price; many places south-east of London, like Lewisham and Penge, saw dreadful loss of life and the destruction of homes and livelihoods.

After the war, the London County Council expanded further into the countryside to build homes for Londoners displaced by the war, and London's boundaries crept ever further outwards. This growth was reflected in the administrative changes which followed, and also in the attempts to control the growth of the capital by the introduction of green belt land around it.

In 1963 the Local Government Act replaced the London County Council with the Greater London Council, which established a number of London boroughs from former metropolitan boroughs in and around London, including Kent. The south-east London boroughs formed from the old administrative county of Kent included Greenwich, Lewisham, Bexley and Bromley. In 1986 the Conservative government abolished the Labour-dominated GLC. At the start of the 21st century, the Labour government established a new controlling body, the Greater London Authority; for the first time Greater London had its own mayor, when Londoners elected the former head of the GLC, Ken Livingstone, to the post.

In 2003, south-east London continues to feel the pressure of an expanding population and new waves of immigration, along with increasing demand for affordable housing. This book opens a window on the past century of change in South-East London.

BROMLEY, *High Street 1899* 42935

13

THE HEART OF A MARITIME NATION: GREENWICH

GREENWICH

GREENWICH'S name derives from the Saxon 'greena-wic', meaning 'green creek'. For centuries the Thames-side location was a favourite with English kings and queens. The Greenwich waterfront is now a World Heritage site; the historic buildings here include the Queen's House, built by Inigo Jones in the early 17th century (the model for the White House in Washington DC in America), the Royal Observatory, founded by Charles II in 1675 (the location of the Prime Meridian since 1884), and the Old Royal Naval College, originally the Seamen's Hospital, commissioned by William and Mary in 1694.

In 1900 the Metropolitan Boroughs of Greenwich and Woolwich were created, and in 1965 these two boroughs amalgamated to form the London Borough of Greenwich. In 2000 the Millennium Dome was built on the Greenwich Peninsula, and the area around Greenwich has been the focus of significant development in recent years. Its maritime and military heritage attracts thousands of visitors annually.

▲ **GREENWICH,** *Royal College Promenade 1951* G204010

In the foreground is the riverside walk along the front of the Old Naval College. On the right is a red granite obelisk commemorating the young French explorer, Joseph Rene Bellot (1826-1853). He took part in two expeditions to find traces of Sir John Franklin, who died in his attempt to discover the North-West Passage, the Arctic sea route linking the Atlantic with the Pacific. After his death the memorial was erected by public subscription. The inscription reads: 'To the intrepid young Bellot of the French Navy who in the endeavour to rescue Franklin, shared the fate and the glory of that illustrious navigator - from his British admirers 1853'. At the rear we can see the chimneys of Greenwich power station, built in 1902-10 for the London County Council to provide electric power to the capital's tramways.

◄ **GREENWICH,** *The Naval College 1951* G204288

The Old Royal Naval College was founded by William and Mary in 1694 as a hospital 'for the relief and support of seamen and their dependants and for the improvement of navigation'. The site was planned by Sir Christopher Wren, and the buildings were designed by Hawksmoor and Vanbrugh in the early part of the 18th century. The Painted Ceiling in the Great Hall by Sir James Thornhill is particularly admired; it was here that Nelson lay in state in 1806. The Hospital was closed in 1869, and in 1873 the buildings became the Royal Naval College. In 1998 the Royal Navy left Greenwich, and the site was handed over to the Greenwich Foundation. In 1999 the University of Greenwich started teaching there, and it was joined in October 2001 by Trinity College of Music.

GREENWICH, *Wolfe's Statue c1955* G204029

The statue of General James Wolfe (1727-59) by Robert Tait McKenzie looks out over the Thames in Greenwich Park. The statue was erected in 1930, and bears the inscription: 'This monument, a gift of the Canadian people, was unveiled by the Marquis de Montcalm'. General Wolfe commanded the British forces at Quebec against the French, and won a great victory at the cost of his life. He was a resident of Greenwich, and is buried in the parish church, St Alfege's.

ELTHAM

ELTHAM was historically a small market town eight miles south-east of London on the road to Maidstone. A popular spot with the Plantagent kings in the Middle Ages, who built Eltham Palace there, it fell out of royal favour with Queen Elizabeth I. In the 17th century, during the Commonwealth, the palace was largely destroyed (apart from the Great Hall). Shooters Hill, running through Eltham Common, was used to display the bodies of executed highwaymen, with the last execution taking place in 1805. The village street near the palace and the surrounding land remained rural until Archibald Cameron Corbett bought the Eltham Park Estate and developed it for suburban housing between 1900 and 1914.

The growing workforce at the Royal Arsenal at nearby Woolwich, the development of public housing, the arrival of the railways and the construction of the Shooters Hill by-pass all led to further growth in the inter-war years. Today it is in the London Borough of Greenwich.

ELTHAM, *Eltham Palace c1960* E33056

The two main surviving structures at the palace, the Great Hall and the moat bridge, were built around the end of the 15th century. When Stephen and Virginia Courtauld moved to Eltham in the 1930s, they restored the surviving structures and built Courtauld House, a stunning Art Deco building, alongside. The superbly restored house and the original Hall are run by English Heritage and open to the public.

ELTHAM, *Well Hall Pleasaunce Gardens c1960* E33063

Close to Eltham Palace, beside the road to Woolwich, lay the medieval estate of Well Hall, which was also moated. The main house, of which no record survives, stood in the centre of the moat. The Tudor barn, the moat, and the garden walls survive, but the original house within the moat, and its 18th-century successor, has disappeared. The later Well Hall House was home to the children's writer Edith Nesbit from 1899 to 1921. In 1960 Well Hall Pleasaunce was an attractive public space with many interesting features, including a bowling green (seen here), thatched pavilions, a 1930s garden, an Italian garden and a cascade. Lack of funding contributed to a decline in the late 20th century. However the Pleasaunce was restored in 2001 with £2.7 million of Lottery funding.

ELTHAM, *The Winter Garden, Avery Hill c1960* E33047

In the late 19th century the house and estate at Avery Hill were leased to 'Colonel' John North, 'the Nitrate King', who had made his fortune in South America. North spared no expense in upgrading the property, and added a Turkish bath, a fernery, a conservatory and a huge dome-covered winter garden. After his early death, the house and 28 acres of parkland were purchased in 1902 by the LCC for £25,000. Four years later it opened as Avery Hill College, the first residential training college for (women) teachers. The 100ft-square winter garden is the best surviving example in London. The structure has been restored from the decay shown in the photograph, and the statues and plants offer a spectacular display of Victorian engineering and gardening at its height. Today is it part of the University of Greenwich, and open to the public.

▶ **ELTHAM**
High Street c1960 E33078

We are looking down the hill. The Royal Arsenal Co-operative is on the left corner opposite Dolcis shoe shop on the right, which is next to Hinds department store. The wide street contains a varied range of shops and parked cars.

▼ **ELTHAM**
High Street 1961 E33069

We see the High Street from the approach up Eltham Hill. This view is little changed today, although the trees are much larger. On the left, beyond the modern Esso garage, is the parish church of St John the Baptist. The earliest church on the site dated back to 1120. The current building, designed by Sir Arthur Blomfield and consecrated in 1875, replaced a 17th-century church on the site.

◄ **ELTHAM**
High Street 2003
E33701

In 2003 the Co-op is still there on the left, but in a rebuilt shop. The large ugly 1960s building on the right also survives. The four gabled houses beyond it, however, have been demolished, and in 2003 this was a vacant building lot. The rest of the High Street has changed little, and remains a mixture of the old and new.

► **ELTHAM**
Well Hall Road c1960
E33066A

▼ **ELTHAM**
Well Hall Road c1960
E33060A

Well Hall Road is on the Progress Estate, which was built in 1915 for workers at the nearby Woolwich Arsenal. The architect was Sir Frank Baines, who built the houses in a range of styles based on the 'garden suburb' architectural trend of that time.

REBUILDING AFTER THE BLITZ: LEWISHAM

LEWISHAM

THE name Lewisham derives from the Old English 'ham', meaning 'a village', and was probably named for the site of 'Leof's village'. It is sited at the confluence of the Ravensbourne and Quaggy rivers (near the existing bus station). The 1086 Domesday Book refers to 'Levesham' having 11 mills.

Before the Industrial Revolution the local mills were used for grinding steel for weapons and for tanning leather, as well as for grinding corn. Lewisham became a popular country location for rich city men from the 17th century onwards; at this time the village of Lewisham stretched along Lewisham High Street from the present railway station to the ancient parish church of St Mary, rebuilt in 1774. The population increased rapidly after the first railway opened in 1849 and the upper classes moved here during the 19th century. By 1900 there were a number of large shops in the town centre.

During World War II nearly 3,000 residents were killed, 8,000 injured and over 68,000 made homeless. Nearly every single school, church, shop and public building was damaged or destroyed. The town centre was devastated by a flying bomb in 1944. A series of air-raid shelters has recently been found under Lewisham High Street.

In 1965 it gave its name to the new London Borough of Lewisham. In 1977 the new shopping centre was built, and in 1994 the High Street was pedestrianised. The Town Centre was reorganised in the mid 1990s to alleviate the traffic congestion, and the arrival of the Docklands Light Railway in the late 1990s caused further changes. In 2003 developers were invited to compete for a massive redevelopment and regeneration project to revitalise a large area of land between Lewisham town centre and the bus, rail and DLR stations.

LEWISHAM, *The Parish Church of St Mary c1960* L373019

The present church was built in 1774-1777 on the site of earlier churches. Gibson's design incorporated the 15th-century tower (1471-1512) of the medieval church and a portico, much admired for its lightness and beauty. A fire in 1830 seriously damaged the north side of the church. The chancel, designed by Sir Arthur Blomfield, was added in 1881 when the nave was re-modelled in Victorian style.

LEWISHAM
*Ladywell Recreation Ground
c1960* L373006

Ladywell was originally a settlement to the west of the High Street between Lewisham and Catford. It took its name from a holy well dedicated to the Virgin Mary, like the nearby parish church. Ladywell Fields, formerly known as Ladywell Recreation Ground, were local water-meadows, purchased to be a public open space in 1889. The land had to be drained before it could be used, and a series of bridges were built over the Ravensbourne. It retains the same appearance today, although like many modern parks, it suffers from lack of maintenance.

LEWISHAM, *High Street c1960* L373009

This view was taken looking up the High Street from Ladywell, with the parish church of St Mary the Virgin behind the trees on the left. St Mary's church hall is opposite.

LEWISHAM
High Street c1960
L373013

This view looks up
Loampit Vale towards
Lewisham station.
Chiesman's department
store, later acquired by
the House of Fraser group,
can be seen behind and to
the left of the clock tower.
Chiesman's was
demolished in the 1990's
and a new police station
now occupies the site. The
clock tower was
completed in 1900 to
celebrate the Diamond
Jubilee of Queen Victoria
in 1897. The Royal Arsenal
Co-op on the extreme
right is now Yates' wine
bar. The modern
pedestrianised shopping
centre is to the right of the
picture.

CATFORD

LOCAL tradition has it that Catford is named after the wild cats who lived next to the ford across the River Ravensbourne here, a tradition continued today by the Catford Cat - a 10ft model black cat crouched over the entrance to Catford's shopping arcade. Historically there were farms and mills here, and the inhabitants of the hamlet Rushey Green fished and sailed on the river Ravensbourne. In 1857 a station for the Mid Kent railway line was built at Catford Bridge, and further development took place in the 1890s when the Forsters, Lewisham's largest landowners, began to develop their farmland south of Catford.

Catford was badly damaged during the Second World War and haphazardly improved afterwards. Continuing uncertainty about the final route of the South Circular Road prevented major redevelopment, and central Catford today is a loud, untidy London outpost on the South Circular road. It is the administrative centre for the London Borough of Lewisham, which has its town hall here.

▲ **CATFORD,** *Bromley Road* 2003 C520701

This is the same view as C520001. The parade of shops has
survived, and so has the bus garage opposite them. The
familiar London double-decker buses can be seen in the
distance. There are now railings along the road edge, and a new
pelican crossing. The attractive parade of symmetrical shops
on the right still exists. While Henkel's on the corner is now a
Chicago Hot Pizza parlour, two doors along at number 231 the
Bromley Road Hardware stores is still there, and still with its
original pre-war interior. Visit it while you can! The United
Dairies is now a Vantage pharmacy.

◀ **CATFORD,** *Bromley Road* c1960 C520001

We are looking up Bromley Road in Bellingham, at the southern
end of Catford. The roof of the bus garage can be seen on the
left just beyond the traffic lights. On the right-hand side is a
United Dairies, and on the other side of Daneby Road we can
see Henkel's bakery and the Bromley Road hardware stores.

29

CATFORD
Peter Pan's Playground
c1955 C520009

Mountsfield Park was opened in August 1905 following the acquisition of Mountsfield, the former house of Henry Stainton. The park is in Hither Green, just east of Catford town centre. An adult is driving the small train round the track, while a mother looks on watchfully in the background, probably keeping an eye on the three lads in the foreground. Mountsfield Park today is the venue for the annual Lewisham People's Day.

CATFORD, *Southend Road c1955* C520012

This is the junction of Southend Road and Catford Road, south of the modern Catford town centre. The trees on the left now cover the entrance gates to Catford Wanderers sports ground. The tram service was extended from Catford to Southend in 1914, but Southend itself, at the southern end of Catford, remained isolated in farmland until the 1920s, when the London County Council housing estates were built on either side of the village. Just round the corner, the old mill pond now lies in front of the modern Homebase DIY store.

FOREST HILL

FOREST Hill is one of the highest hills in London. As a place, it did not exist until the late 18th century, when woodland on the edge of Sydenham Common started to be developed for housing and was given the name of Forest Hill. The new railway station, which opened at the foot of the hill in 1839, was originally called The Dartmouth Arms, after the local hostelry. The wooded slopes of the hill, however, soon attracted wealthy owners, who built large houses there. In 1845 the new station was renamed Forest Hill, and the original Forest Hill area to the north changed its name to Honor Oak, after a tree on One Tree Hill, where Queen Elizabeth I is believed to have picnicked on May Day in 1602. The centre of Forest Hill, now in the London Borough of Lewisham, is now a conservation area.

FOREST HILL, *The Horniman Museum c1950* F179003

The distinctive rounded tower of the Horniman Museum is a familiar sight to travellers on the London Road, the A205 (South Circular). A Number 58 electric tram from Dulwich to the Blackwall Tunnel via Lordship Lane (the A221) can be seen making its way over the crest of the hill. The trams ceased running on October 6, 1951. Frederick Horniman was a wealthy Quaker tea merchant, who lived in Forest Hill in the late 19th and early 20th century. An inveterate traveller, he amassed large collections of natural history, arts and handicrafts from all around the world. At one stage, Mrs Horniman is believed to have issued an ultimatum: either the collections must go, or she would. Mr Horniman responded by building a museum to house the collection, which he donated to the public in 1901. The Horniman Museum is currently undergoing a £10 million renovation and expansion.

FOREST HILL
London Road c1950
F179001

This view was taken from outside Forest Hill station at the foot of the hill looking up London Road. The Number 62 electric tram between Lordship Lane and East Dulwich has just rounded the corner. The Capitol cinema on the left is still there today, now a J D Wetherspoon pub conversion. The café and shops on the left are now combined to form a Blockbuster Video store.

FOREST HILL
London Road c1955
F179014

This view looks down the hill towards Forest Hill railway station at the bottom. The shops on the left as far as the tobacconist's were empty and boarded up in the summer of 2003. The shop next to the parked car is currently a branch of the MacDonald's hamburger chain. The tram tracks are still visible in the road.

▶ **FOREST HILL**
Christ Church 1898 42674

Christ Church, formerly the parish church of Forest Hill, was built between 1852 and 1885 on a site given by the Earl of Dartmouth, who wanted an imposing centrepiece for the Dartmouth estate. The architect was Ewan Christian. The Grade II listed building was declared redundant in July 2003; it is due to be converted into residential accommodation, with a small place of worship created in the chancel.

▼ **FOREST HILL**
The Children's Pool, Horniman Gardens c1955
F179004

Open-air paddling pools for children were very popular in the 1950s. The Horniman museum is surrounded by extensive gardens, which were originally part of Frederick Horniman's Surrey Mount home.

ROMAN ROADS LEAD TO LONDON: BEXLEY

ERITH

ERITH is eight miles from London, and lies on rising ground on the south bank of the River Thames just west of where it meets the River Darent. The town dates back to Saxon times, when the name Erith meant 'muddy harbour'. Henry VII built a royal dockyard here in the 16th century near the modern Riverside Gardens.

A popular venue for a day out by river for Londoners in the late 19th century, The Pier Hotel and riverside gardens, whose attractions included a maze and arboretum, attracted day trippers from London in their thousands. By 1901 Erith had grown to over 25,000 inhabitants, and flour milling had developed as a major industry. During World War II, Erith was the site of engineering and munitions factories, and was heavily bombed. As if this was not enough, in the mid 1960s the town centre's surviving Victorian buildings were demolished and replaced by modern architecture in a major reconstruction project. Today Erith is in the London Borough of Bexley.

ERITH, *High Street c1950* E58012

► **ERITH**
High Street c1953
E58014

Originally Erith was composed of two streets, one leading down to the waterside, the other branching off to the left towards the church. In this photograph, the distinctive shop front of Burton's the tailors (right) faces Hedley Mitchell's department store (left.) Mitchell's closed in 1961 after 150 years in business in the town. A large Union Jack hangs up at the end of the street, possibly to mourn the death of George VI or to celebrate the ascension of the young Elizabeth II. The old shops were swept away in the redevelopment of the mid 1960s.

◄ **ERITH**
High Street c1965 E58041

The early fascias of the familiar high street stores Boots and Dolcis can be now seen on the right of the street. A Triumph Herald car is parked outside Boots. Note the two 'rockers' on the left of the picture crossing the road. A sign of increasing prosperity is the D.I.Y shop called 'contemporary home decor' on the left, with a window full of wallpaper.

ERITH
The Thames c1950
E58022

In the mid-19th century the ships of the East India Company took advantage of the open access to the upper part of the Long Reach, when proceeding up the river, to discharge part of their cargo and to receive ballast when going down river. In recent years the old deep wharfe has been redeveloped and the town now has a new river front and pier.

ERITH, *Pier Road c1950* E58017

The frontage of the town's original department store, Hedley Mitchell, can be seen on the right on its corner site. There is little traffic to be seen. Like the rest of Erith, Pier Road underwent extensive redevelopment in the 1960s, with many Victorian buildings being replaced by the concrete blocks of modern architecture popular with architects and planners at the time.

BEXLEYHEATH

UNTIL it was enclosed in 1819, Bexley Heath was rough heathland alongside the London to Dover road, frequented by highwaymen. The earliest settlement, called Bexley New Town, spread out along the main road in the area known as the Broadway. William Morris and Philip Webb built their celebrated Red House in Bexleyheath in 1860, and the railway arrived in 1895. The surrounding countryside was urbanised extensively in the 1930s. Since the 1980s the town centre has been redeveloped around a large shopping mall, the Broadway Centre. Today, Bexleyheath is the main administrative base for the London Borough of Bexley.

BEXLEYHEATH
The Clock Tower c1950 B650022

The clock tower which stands in the centre of the shopping centre was erected to commemorate King George V's coronation in 1911. Designed by W M Eppas, it cost £590, and the foundation stone was laid in 1912. In the west alcove is a bust of King George V, and in the east alcove (a 1997 addition) a bust of William Morris. The Number 696 trolley bus in the photograph ran from Woolwich to Bexleyheath Market Place via Welling.

43

BEXLEYHEATH
The Broadway c1960
B650041

On the right is Townley Road. The shopping centre here has been extensively redeveloped and pedestrianised since this photograph was taken. The monolithic Broadway shopping centre was developed between Townley Road and Pincott Road, and opened by the Duke of Edinburgh in 1984. The second stage opened in 2001.

BEXLEYHEATH
Pickford Lane c1950
B650011

Bexleyheath railway station is in Pickford Lane to the west of the town centre. At the start of the 1930s the town was still concentrated along Watling Street, and Pickford Lane was still in rural countryside. By the end of the decade new estates were being laid out; the Brampton Park Estate was built by D C Bowyer in the countryside between the former lanes of Brampton Road and Pickford Lane.

BEXLEYHEATH, *Watling Street c1950*   B650023

Watling Street was the old Roman road from London to Canterbury and Dover, nowadays the A207, which runs through the centre of modern Bexleyheath. The extensive network of trolley bus cables which then covered London are clearly visible here. In 1935 Bexleyheath Garage was established as the first purpose-built garage in London for trolley buses. The trolley buses stopped running in 1959.

BEXLEYHEATH, *Barnehurst Road c1960* B650077

Barnehurst grew up in the 1930s around Barnehurst railway
station one mile east of Bexleyheath centre. This photograph
was taken from the road where it crosses the railway line. Note
the newspaper seller's box in the right foreground near the
station entrance. The Red Barn Hotel (right) still exists today.
In the middle distance are Bursted Woods.

BEXLEY

IN THE 5TH CENTURY, Bexley in Kent was known as Byxlea, 'the settlement among the box trees'. At the time of the Domesday Book, it was inhabited by 41 villagers, 15 smallholders, and 100 pigs, and it had a church and 3 mills. Market gardening and agriculture were the main sources of income locally, until the railway arrived in 1886 and swept up the surrounding areas into London's urban sprawl.

BEXLEY
The Parish Church of St Mary the Virgin
c1955 B83008

There has been a church here for over 800 years. The present church is Early English in style with a typical Kentish shingled spire. The interior was heavily restored by the Victorians in 1883, and the lych gate was repaired in 1983 with the aid of a Council Heritage grant.

BEXLEY
Hall Place c1960
B83054

Hall Place is a Grade I listed Tudor/Jacobean house on the banks of the river Cray; its origins go back to 1241. Lady Limerick, who lived here from 1917 to 1943, began the celebrated topiary in the gardens. Hall Place today includes a local museum, and both the house and grounds are open to the public.

BEXLEY, *The Black Prince Public House c1950* B83017

Legend has it that Edward, the Black Prince, lived at nearby Hall Place in the 14th century. In 1944 the pub was home to senior members of the US 'Ultra' code-breaking team. In the 1970s it was a popular live venue for rock groups, including Eric Clapton, Roxy Music and the Rolling Stones. Today, its appearance unchanged, it is marooned on a vast traffic island, the infamous Black Prince interchange, where the A2, the A220 and the A223 meet. A Holiday Inn hotel was built alongside it in 2001.

▼ **BEXLEY,** *The Old Mill c1965* B83063

There has been a mill here, where Bexley High Street crosses the River Cray, since the 11th century. The last mill on the site, built in the 18th century, burned down in a mysterious fire in 1966, and this photograph must be one of the last taken of the building. Since then, the mill has been rebuilt in traditional style, and today it is a restaurant and public house.

► **BEXLEY**
High Street c1955
B83040

This view was taken looking up Bexley High Street towards the junction with Bourne Road. The railway bridge can be seen in the distance. The river Cray goes under the road here, and the rebuilt mill is just round the corner on the left. The cottages on the right are still there, unchanged, today.

◄ **BEXLEY**
High Street c1965
B83065

We are looking east along the High Street to its junction with Bourne Road on the left; The King's Head public house, on the left, dates back to the 16th century.

► **BEXLEY**
High Street 2003
B83701

This is the same view as B83065. Today it is Henry VIII's head on the pub sign. The Robin Hood cleaners' shop on the right has become the Bon Appetit sandwich bar. At the end of the two buildings are now the Viceroy of India restaurant (left) and an Internet-based financial services company (right).

SIDCUP

SIDCUP grew up around The Black Horse pub (now called The Blue Rose) in the High Street. In the 13th century it was Cetecopp, 'the fold in the hill'. In the 18th century, the pleasant countryside and plentiful springs attracted wealthy landowners who built their country houses in the area, including Lamorbey, Sidcup Place and Foots Cray. The railway arrived in the town in 1865 - a station was built one mile north of the town on the edge of Lamorbey Park, next to the hamlet of Halfway Street.

In the late 1920s and early 1930s, developers like New Ideal Homesteads Ltd bought up large tracts of land that had formerly been part of the great estates, and built large housing developments. In World War II the area was under the route of German bombers targeting central London, and was badly damaged, particularly by V2 rockets in 1944-45. Since 1965 it has been part of the London Borough of Bexley.

SIDCUP
High Street c1965 s127105

This photograph was taken looking up Main Road from the junction with Station Road and the High Street. The building with the stone porch on the right is the original Victorian police station. Lyle's Lemonade van is proceeding up the street; the parade of shops behind has a range of fascias, but most of the names are obscured by the blinds to protect the contents of the windows from the sun.

SIDCUP
High Street 2003
S127701

This is the same view as S127105. The police station is still occupied by the police today. The rest of the parade is little altered, although the shops reflect contemporary interests: Gilbert's is now Sun Lee Chinese fast food, while George Summer's is Sidcup Dry Cleaners, and other shops include the Moghul Indian restaurant and an Internet café. The blinds have gone.

SIDCUP, *Station Road c1955* S127093

Sidcup railway station is about one mile north of Sidcup on the outskirts of Lamorbey Park. The railway station buildings are to the far left. The houses at the far end of the shops on the right have been replaced by a modern office block. The parade of shops remains, and today includes the Co-op undertaker's, a greetings card shop and Machin's bakeries. In 2003 the middle three shops were being converted into a Tesco Metro food store.

SIDCUP, *The Oval c1955* S127060

The Oval is two miles north of Sidcup in the Blackfen area. This parade of shops is on New Ideal Homesteads' Marlborough Park estate, which was built in the 1930s. Current shops in the Oval include Olin's Pharmacy, the Oval Pets Centre, DIY shops and an Indian brasserie. In front is an ornamental grassed area with roses, bedding plants and trees.

SIDCUP
*The Baptist
Chapel and
Public Hall
1900* 45816

SIDCUP, *Lamorbey Park c1960* S127019

Lamorbey House, an 18th-century mansion, was occupied by Kent College for the Careers Service from 1948 to 1973. In the photograph a class can be seen taking place on the lawns. In 2003 it is occupied by the Rose Bruford College for Theatre Studies.

SIDCUP, *Frognal Avenue 1900* 45822

Frognal House, whose lodge gates are seen here, was the home of
Lord Sydney in the 18th century. The rural character of the area -
notice the horse and trap ambling along in the middle distance -
has long since gone. Frognal House is now in the grounds of
Queen Mary's Hospital. Most recently it has been an old
people's home.

BROMLEY, *A View from the Recreation Ground 1898* 42940

LEAFY SUBURBS LOOK TO THE SKIES: BROMLEY

BROMLEY

BROMLEY is first recorded in AD 862 as Bromleag, meaning 'clearing where the broom grows'. The river Ravensbourne runs through Bromley to Deptford Creek from its source in nearby Keston. Its early importance was due to the presence of the Bishop of Rochester's palace (now the core of the civic offices) and its weekly market. A medicinal well in the grounds of the palace enabled it to flourish briefly as a spa town in the 19th century. However, after the bishops moved out in 1844 and the palace was sold, the town marked time until the arrival of the railways in 1858.

Following redevelopment in the 1930s the town suffered from bombing in World War II, the High Street birthplace of the author H G Wells being a casualty. In 1965 Bromley and its surrounding areas became the London Borough of Bromley. The town now has a bustling shopping centre, The Glades, and the main part of the old High Street and Market Square have been pedestrianised.

BROMLEY
High Street 1899 42935

The original shops on the
High Street show that
Bromley was a prosperous
and busy town. The elegant
stores, which include a
music shop, a men's
outfitters and a butcher's,
are lit by gas lamps and
have pavement displays –
note the rabbits hanging up
outside the butcher's (right).
Horses and traps are
proceeding down the centre
of the High Street.

BROMLEY, *High Street 1948* B226008

In 1948 the influence of post-war austerity was still strong, as can be seen in the poster on the left exhorting everyone to recycle their waste. A London country bus - destination Sevenoaks - is proceeding down the centre of the street. This part of the High Street is pedestrianised today, and only the local jeweller's, E W Payne, remains on its centre site at the top of the street. A blue plaque on Allders department store opposite commemorates its predecessor, Medhurst's. Otherwise the old shops have been swept away by the big High Street chains like Next, The Body Shop, BHS and Marks & Spencer.

BROMLEY
Market Square c1950
B226011

The market square was originally redeveloped in 1863, when a town hall was erected. In 1933 the old Town Hall and island shops were demolished and replaced by a mock Tudor block (right). The portico on the butcher's, W F Skilton (left), protected customers arriving by carriage from the elements. On the far side of the square are Isaac Walton (men's outfitters), A B Hemmings and W Dell (seedsmen and corn dealers).

BROMLEY, *Market Square 2003* B226701

Shops here today serve a more urban clientele than in 1950, and include MacDonald's (the burger chain), mcv (music and electronic games), and Jessop's camera shop. The shops on the far side have been replaced by Café Rouge, Zucchi and the Abbey National building society. A mural commemorates the birthplace of the novelist H G Wells at 46 High Street in 1866. The area to the right is now pedestrianised, and leads to the Glades shopping centre.

BROMLEY
High Street c1950
B226002

This photograph was taken from the southern end of the High Street. As yet, however, there seems to be little traffic. The Gaumont cinema, which opened in 1936, closed down in 1961 and is now a Habitat store. The Glades shopping centre, yet to be built, now covers a large area on the right of the photograph further up the high street.

▶ **BROMLEY**
Library Gardens
c1955 B226047

▼ **BROMLEY**
Library Gardens
c1955 B226029

Elaborate formal carpet bedding schemes were popular in municipal gardens in the post war years, and floral clocks, like the one shown here in the Library Gardens behind the Churchill theatre, were a demonstration of the gardener's art.

BECKENHAM

BECKENHAM appears in the Domesday Book of 1086 as 'Bacheham', 'Beohha's village'. Ten miles from London Bridge, the area has long been popular with wealthy Londoners: in the 16th century the Duke of Suffolk entertained Henry VIII at Beckenham Manor House, and in the 18th century the Quaker timber merchant John Cator became lord of the manor and built Beckenham Place. His descendants developed the surrounding estate for 'superior' housing in the 19th century, and following the arrival of the railway in 1857 the town grew continuously. Today it is part of the London Borough of Bromley.

BECKENHAM, *Beckenham Place 1899* 43383

John Cator purchased the local manor house in 1773, and renovated it with the wing and portico from Wricklemarsh House, Blackheath. After being inhabited by a succession of private tenants in the 19th century, the house became a boys' school and later a sanatorium. In 1907 the park was leased to Beckenham Golf Club, who built the first golf course there; in 1927 the park and mansion were acquired by the London County Council. During World War II it housed Italian prisoners of war, and the open space was turned over to allotments. Today Beckenham Place Park is a public park with one of England's largest and busiest public golf courses (administered by the London Borough of Lewisham). The Grade II mansion includes a café and bar, and there is a visitor centre run by the Friends of Beckenham Place Park, which is open at weekends.

BECKENHAM
Church Hill 1899 43377

Originally, the upper part of the High Street here was called Church Hill. A gas lamp can be seen on the left side of the road - gas lighting locally was supplied by the Crystal Palace District Gas Company. A woman (possibly a nanny) is pushing a baby in a traditional baby carriage up the hill. St George's church at the top of the hill dates back to the 14th century, and its 13th-century lych gate is believed to be the oldest in England. The current church was rebuilt in 1857. In this photograph it has no tower, as this was not completed until 1903.

BECKENHAM, *Church Hill c1955* B46020

Little has changed here from the 1899 photograph apart from the arrival of road markings and traffic lights. St George's church now has its familiar tower. T W Thornton, whose premises can be seen on the left, was a local benefactor and publisher of the weekly Beckenham Journal and a local trade directory. Today the building is occupied by estate agents, and an adjacent Thornton's shop lies vacant. Tom William Thornton (1857-1913) was a prominent local citizen; in 1902, with Dr Francis Barton, a local GP, he hired a huge balloon filled with coal gas to commemorate the coronation of King Edward VII and Queen Alexandra. They flew over Kent dropping bags of mail, before crossing the English Channel to land on the beach near Calais. In 1913 Tom Thornton was instrumental in acquiring Kelsey Park for the local community.

BECKENHAM, *The Town Hall and Parish Church c1950* B46006

BECKENHAM, *Elm Road Chapel 1899* 43391

Elm Road Baptist Chapel, which opened in 1883, was designed by Edward Mountfield, the architect of the Old Bailey. The houses around it were part of the same development. The celebrated 20th-century children's novelist Enid Blyton (1897-1968) grew up in Beckenham and attended the chapel. Her best friend was Mary Attenborough, an aunt of Richard and David Attenborough; Mary's father supervised the Sunday School. Enid was baptised there when she was 13 years old.

BECKENHAM
High Street c1965
B46075

Next to Beckenham Toys on the right is a very early branch of Tesco, alongside the Co-operative Building Society. A London country bus is proceeding down the middle of the High Street.

BECKENHAM, *High Street 2003* B46701

This is the same view as B46075. Beckenham Toys is still in business, now next door to the shop it occupied in 1965. The parade of shops on the left has survived, including the mock-Tudor gabled shops in the middle distance. Just out of the picture on the left opposite the level crossing is The Three Tuns public house, one of the oldest inns in Beckenham. In the summer of 2003 this was closed and facing an uncertain future.

PENGE

PENGE is a Celtic word meaning 'hill in the forest'. The 1086 Domesday Book refers to Penge as having 'a wood for fifty hogs pannage' with woodland pasture 'seven miles, seven furlongs and seven feet in circumference'.

The forest was the Great North Wood that covered much of the area to the north of Croydon. Never a parish in its own right, Penge was historically part of the Manor of Battersea 12 miles away.

Development began after the common was enclosed and plots sold off for building in 1827.

In 1854 Joseph Paxton selected the area to re-locate the Crystal Palace from Hyde Park. The London & Brighton Railway built a line and a station to serve the Palace so that by 1861 the area had developed and the population rose to 5015. By 1871 it was a town with a population of 13201 and by 1900 Penge was in reality a suburb of London

Over the years Penge has moved from Surrey to Kent and back again. In 1965 it became part of the London Borough of Bromley.

PENGE, *The Royal Naval Asylum c1960* P26007

The King William IV Royal Naval Asylum in St. John's Road, founded in the 1840s, was paid for by Queen Adelaide to provide accommodation for the widows of naval officers. Designed by Philip Hardwicke in a Tudor style, it has now been converted into private residences.

PENGE, *The Watermen's and Lightermen's Almshouses c1965* P26012

The Watermen's and Lightermen's Almshouses were built to provide accommodation for retired freemen of the Company of Watermen and Lightermen and their widows. Watermen had the job of ferrying people across the Thames in the days when there was only a single bridge; lightermen were pilots taking goods from large ocean-going ships into port, using small boats or lighters. The first stone was laid in May 1840 by Lord Mayor of London, Sir Chapman Marshall, and in 1841, 34 married men, 10 unmarried men, and 32 widows became the almshouses' first residents. They are now private homes.

▶ PENGE
High Street c1965
P26010

On the right the 1960s fascia of Woolworth's can be glimpsed. The shops on the left include Gem's television shop with a 'contemporary' style mosaic entrance wall, next to Richel's 'Hair Artists', both in a typically 1960's brutal concrete parade. The older shop fronts opposite have survived today, although there is now a new shopping centre, the Blenheim Centre, off the High Street.

◀ PENGE
High Street c1965
P26011

The familiar Burtons building can be seen on the right – there are still many surviving branches in this style around south-east London, including the one at Lewisham. On the left, Curtess' shoeshop is next to Kennedy's fish shop alongside Kennedy's sausages. Flower baskets have appeared on the lamp posts.

▲ **PENGE,** *Queen Adelaide's Court c1960* P26006

Queen Adelaide's Court is a 1930s block of municipal flats. The balconies and mature trees are typical of the careful design which the LCC's architects applied to inter-war public housing.

◄ **PENGE**
The Gardens c1960
P26008

In the centre stands the church of St John the Evangelist. Penge was without a church until the building of St John's, although a chapel had existed since 1837. In 1848 John Dudin Brown, who had already donated land for the Watermen's Almhouses, gave a plot in what is now the High Street for the new church. London's micro-climate is already developing by 1960, as can be seen from the sub-tropical cordylines flourishing in the flower-bed.

BIGGIN HILL, *The Airport c1960* B705075

The airfield at Biggin Hill developed during World War I as a test site for
aircraft radio communications. It owes its international reputation to the
crucial role it played in defending London from attack in the Battle of
Britain during World War II. In this photo an Esso tanker is being used to fill
up a small bi-plane on the airfield. In 1958 the station ceased to be an active
base and became primarily a civil airfield; the RAF finally moved out in
1992. A new passenger terminal now allows large passenger charter planes
to land, and it has been renamed London Biggin Hill Airport. A popular air
show is held at Biggin Hill every year.

BIGGIN HILL

BIGGIN Hill, 19 miles from London, is best known for Biggin Hill airfield, which played a vital role in the Battle of Britain. Biggin Hill itself did not exist until the end of the 19th century, when the local manor estate of Aperfield was purchased at auction by an Irish businessman, Frederick Henry Dougal (1849-1904). Dougal sub-divided the land for sale as cheap lots, and promoted the area energetically, naming his new town Biggin Hill, after a local farm (the name is believed to be Middle English in origin, meaning 'the hill next to the farm or dwelling place'). By 1900, Biggin Hill was a small settlement of around 500 people living at the side of the Westerham Road and around the junction with Jail Lane by The Black Horse Inn.

Dougal died at the end of 1904, and development slowed owing to poor access to the area and covenants placed on the land by his trustees. In 1916 the Royal Flying Corps identified the high flat land at Cudham to the north as suitable for testing the then new wireless aviation communications technology. When the Royal Air Force was formed in 1918, the testing station at Cudham evolved into RAF Biggin Hill. Its site was to prove crucial in the defence of London during the Battle of Britain in World War II. The arrival locally of the RAF support staff also caused housing in the surrounding area to expand. A further period of growth took place in the 1960s and 1970s.

▶ **BIGGIN HILL**
Leaves Green c1950 B705003

This was also known in past as Leves Green. The photograph shows The Kings Arms pub on the western edge of Biggin Hill airfield, where Main Road and Leaves Green Road are crossed by Milking Lane, an old track leading to Downe village, now on the other side of the airfield. Its appearance is similar today (2003).

▼ **BIGGIN HILL**
The Fox and Hounds, Westerham Hill c1955 B705008

This was a venue for the Old Surrey Foxhounds to meet in the early 20th century. Biggin Hill was also a popular destination for touring cyclists; the photograph shows a group meeting up outside the pub. Note the sign for local Westerham Ales, brewed by the Black Eagle brewery at Westerham. In 2003 its owners, the brewers Six Continents, announced plans to convert it into an Ember Inn pub-restaurant.

◄**BIGGIN HILL**
Main Road c1960
B705052

The main shopping area of Biggin Hill was restricted to the western side of Main Road by covenants imposed in the early 20th century. The shops shown here are typical of the small group which might serve a community back in the 1950s. This small row of shops still exists (from 190-198 Main Road), although their use has changed to include a florist's, an insurance broker's and a shop selling metal detectors.

BIGGIN HILL, *The Valley c1955* B705022

The 1960s saw further growth locally in the Biggin Hill valley and along and behind Main Road; at this time planning regulations were eased to allow infill development to replace the low density bungalows with higher density modern estates. This photograph captures the old scattered developments before the major developers moved into the area.

CHISLEHURST

THE original settlement at Chislehurst dates back to the Anglo-Saxon period, when the name Ceosol Hyrst meant 'the wood on the gravel'. Pigot's guide of 1840 describes Chislehurst as 'a most respectable village', and the arrival of the railway from New Cross to Chislehurst in 1865 led the village to outgrow its hilltop site 300 feet above sea-level. Today Chislehurst is a scattered village around various commons.

CHISLEHURST *1900* 45825

CHISLEHURST
High Street c1965
C97025

This view looks down the High Street from the top opposite The Queens Head, an old coaching inn recently extensively modernised. This area, Chislehurst West, was historically known as Prickend, and was renamed as the High Street in the early 20th century. The parade of shops on the right remains, although the advertisements for Guinness, Nelson cigarettes and Weekend chocolates have long since disappeared. Today the café is a Chinese restaurant. Further down the hill, the church of the Annunciation of the Blessed Virgin Mary can be seen behind the shops. The church was built in 1868, and was positioned so it would face the early morning sunrise on March 25, the day of the Feast of the Annunciation. The tower was added in 1930. Opposite the church today a large and intrusive red brick Sainsburys superstore now dominates the site, completely out of character with the surrounding area. Also, the churchyard has been badly vandalised.

CHISLEHURST
St Nicholas' Church 1900
45826

The church of St Nicholas is situated on Chislehurst Common, near the junction of Prince Imperial Road and Bromley Road. The flint church, which has an oak shingled spire, contains the tomb of the Walsingham family, who leased the manor from Elizabeth I. Nearby is a memorial to the Prince Imperial, the only son of Empress Eugenie and Napoleon III, who lived nearby at Camden Place (now a golf club) in the late 19th century. The Prince Imperial was killed in the Zulu War in South Africa in 1879.

CHISLEHURST, *Prickend Pond c1965* C97029

The varied geology in the area, including chalk, clay and gravel, has been quarried and mined since medieval times. Like many of the ponds locally, Prickend Pond at the northern end of Chislehurst is a former gravel pit which has filled with water from the numerous local streams. In the photograph the spire of St Nicholas' church can be glimpsed across the trees.

DOWNE

THE village of Downe dates back to the 11th century. Its spelling has varied over the years, from 'Dune' and 'Doune' to 'Down', but it was fixed in the early 20th century as Downe. It prob- ably derives from the old English 'dun', meaning 'hill'. It is chiefly known today for Downe House, the home for many years of the eminent Victorian scientist Charles Darwin (1809-1882).

DOWNE, *The Village c1950* D167016

The Kentish spire of the 13th-century church of St Mary the Virgin can be seen in the middle distance. The church was restored in 1871, and Darwin's wife Emma is buried in the churchyard. The cars lined up outside the church in the photograph suggest that a wedding or funeral is in progress. The east end of the church was damaged by a bomb in World War II, and the east window was completely destroyed. It was rebuilt in 1950. In 1969 a window by Keith Coleborn was given by Mr and Mrs Knox-Johnston, who lived locally, to commemorate the voyage of their son, Robin, in *Suhaili* in 1968, when he became the first man to sail non-stop around the world singlehanded.

▶ **DOWNE**
High Street c1955 D167049

Downe village today attracts a stream of visitors to Downe House, but it remains rural in character. There are two pubs, The George and Dragon and The Queens Head (right), which was adopted as their local by US forces stationed in the area during World War 2. The area also attracted walkers and cyclists; in the middle distance we can see Gee's tea rooms and a lorry delivering Tizer, the popular post-war fizzy drink.

▼ **DOWNE**
Downe House c1950 D167021

Charles Darwin bought Downe House in 1842 for £2200, and moved in with his wife Emma. He had already spent five years in the southern hemisphere voyaging on the *Beagle*, and it was at Downe House that he wrote *The Origin of Species*, which was published in 1859. He lived at Downe House until his death in 1888. Downe House is now run by English Heritage as a memorial museum to his life and work. Together with the nearby Holwood estate, Keston, to the north (home of William Pitt the Younger in the 18th century), it forms part of a proposed World Heritage Site centred on the work of Darwin, who conducted many of his experiments at Holwood.

KESTON

KESTON today is a quiet suburb on the adjoining boundaries of London, Kent and Surrey, north of Biggin Hill. There is evidence of Roman occupation in the area. The Holwood estate was owned by William Pitt the Younger in the late 18th century; he built the manor house, destroying most of the ancient hill fort there. The current Holwood House was built between 1823 and 1826 by Decimus Burton and is Grade I listed - the grounds are Grade II. Holwood now forms part of a proposed World Heritage Site centred on the work of Charles Darwin, who lived nearby at Downe House and who conducted many of his experiments at Holwood. In July 2002, developers applied to build housing on the Holwood estate while at the same time conserving the main house and the historic buildings. This was rejected following a public enquiry.

▲ **KESTON,** *Caesar's Well c1960* K152024

Legend has it that Caesar's Well was found by Roman soldiers
when they were looking for water in the area. They saw a raven
drinking near their camp, and on investigating found a copious
spring. This is the source of the River Ravensbourne, which
eventually discharges into the Thames via Deptford Creek. The
ravens in Bromley's coat of arms represent the Ravensbourne.

◄ **KESTON,** *The Village Green c1960* K152039

Westerham Road, which passes by the ponds, used to be the old
coaching road to Westminster. Keston church, which can be
glimpsed in the middle distance, dates from the 13th century. The
nave of the church turns a little to the north: this is thought to be
due to the belief that the head of Our Lord fell upon his right
shoulder when he died upon the cross. The Greyhound pub
remains a popular pub with walkers and cyclists in the area.

▲ KESTON
The Fishponds c1960 K152007

The Keston fishponds are near the mill. There are three
ponds: one is natural, and the other two are disused
gravel pits which were dammed to form ponds in 1830.
They are fed by the spring known as Caesar's Well.

▶ KESTON
The Mill c1955 K152026A

Keston windmill on the edge of the common is the oldest
surviving windmill in Kent; it is a post mill, and dates
from around 1716. The upper part of the mill rested on a
massive oak centre post, which was rotated by the miller
to ensure the sails faced the wind. Failure to do this
could result in damage to the building. In 1878 a wind hit
the mill and damaged the sails. Part of one was broken
off, and as a precautionary measure, its opposite number
was shortened in order to maintain balance. The upper
structure was renewed and the framework strengthened
in 1913, and it has since undergone further restoration.

WEST WICKHAM

THERE has been a settlement at West Wickham since Roman times. Originally called 'Wickham', from a Saxon word meaning settlement, the 'West' was added to avoid confusion with the other Wickham (now East Wickham) near Welling. West Wickham remained relatively rural until the 1920s. In 1926 the railway was electrified, and after much of the Wickham Court estate was sold off and the developers moved in, West Wickham grew rapidly. Historically part of Kent near the Surrey border, it is now in the London Borough of Bromley.

WEST WICKHAM, *High Street c1955* W601077

A branch of Dewhurst's, the butcher's chain widespread throughout London at the time, can be seen on the left just beyond a branch of the local Co-operative society. Further down is a chemist's. The Swan Hotel on the right is still in business today, offering a weekend disco to its patrons. A London Transport Routemaster is making its way down the High Street, which still has plenty of bicycles, and there is a large queue building up at the bus stop on the right.

WEST WICKHAM
The Coneyhall Estate c1955
W601035

The Coneyhall estate was built in the 1930s by Morrells, the housebuilders, who had bought the Coney Hall farmlands after the death of Sir John Lennard. Morrells were also building new-style 'garden suburbs' at nearby Pett's Wood, a style which can be seen in the many trees and the shrubs along the centre of the road. The parade of shops includes a familiar sight back in the 1950s, the Corn stores next door to A R Theobold the family butcher's. The pillar-box on the pavement denotes a post office under the shop blinds nearby. Local facilities provided for the residents also included the Coneyhall filling station on the left of the photograph.

WEST WICKHAM, *Coloma College c1960* W601095

At the time of this photograph, Coloma College was a teacher training college. Note the topiary birds at the entrance. After the church of the Holy Innocents and orphanage at Orpington was demolished in the late 1970s owing to subsidence, the proceeds were used to convert Coloma College into the St John Rigby School. This hit the headlines in 2003 when the former principal (Colleen McCabe, once a nun) was jailed for 5 years for embezzling half a million pounds from the funds during her time as headmistress.

MOTTINGHAM

MOTTINGHAM was first recorded in AD 862 as 'Modingahema', probably meaning 'the land of Moda's people'. Historically, the main settlement lay along what is now Mottingham Lane. The s urrounding area was farmland. After the arrival of the railway in around 1866, the area began to develop. The West Park area was popular with the middle classes; famous residents included the cricketer W G Grace, who lived in Fairmont, off Mottingham Lane, from 1909 to 1915. In the 1930s the London County Council bought the Court Farm estate, and began building the massive Mottingham estate. After World War 2, Woolwich Council built the Coldharbour estate to the east of Mottingham Road for Londoners made homeless by the Blitz. Mottingham is in the London borough of Bromley, while the Grove Park district to the west is in Lewisham.

MOTTINGHAM, *Court Road c1960* M297005

Still a rural area in the 1930s, by the 1960s this was the view at the junction with Mottingham Road in the area known as Mottingham Village. The parade of shops still existed in 2003, although the Co-op stores has been replaced by a Londis food store, and the sports cycles, toys and games shop is now occupied by Mottingham Motor Cycles.

MOTTINGHAM
Mottingham Road
c1965 M297026

This photograph looks towards the junction with Court Road. In 2003 Hinton's betting shop had become a branch of the William Hill betting shop chain, Cave Austin's grocers had become Edward's photographers, and the other shops had changed hands to include a car accessories shop, a Spar grocer's, and a hairdresser's. In 1965 cigarette advertising was still widespread, in this case for Players and Bristol Tipped cigarettes.

MOTTINGHAM, *The Memorial c1960* M297009

The unusual war memorial, near the junction of Grove Park Road and Mottingham Road, was unveiled in 1920. It was designed by a local resident, George Hubbard, and cost £620. Behind it is a branch of Martins Bank, which was first established in Mottingham at the end of the 19th century. In 1969 Barclays took over Martins, and the branch later closed in the early 1990s. Next to the bank was the Café Mimosa.

MOTTINGHAM
Mottingham Farm Riding School c1965
M297034

Mottingham Farm was worked until the 1950s, producing milk, butter and cheese, but by 1965 it was being used as a riding stables. An early example of product placement is the advertisement for Paul's horse nuts over the stable doors. The riding school is still there today, offering riding lessons to children and young people.

MOTTINGHAM, *The Service Station c1965* M297030

This typical early BP service station with the BP badge logo and attendant-operated petrol pumps was in Mottingham Road. A car wash and toilets were available for the motorist, denoting a superior new petrol station of its time.

► **MOTTINGHAM**
The Recreation Ground c1960
M297003

Many London clubs and colleges have their sports grounds at Mottingham. Here a number of teams are enjoying a game of cricket, although the spectators and waiting players in the foreground are well wrapped up against the English summer weather.

▼ **MOTTINGHAM**
The Chinbrook Public House c1965 M297049

Chinbrook (or Chin Brook) is an alternative name for the River Quaggy. The developments around Chinbrook were built on farmland south-west of Mottingham. Chinbrook Farm on Chinbrook Meadows was a dairy farm. At the end of the 19th century, Chinbrook Road was regarded as a very fashionable street.

◄ **MOTTINGHAM**
*The Prince of
Wales Public
House c1965*
M297032

ORPINGTON

THE town is first recorded in 1032; its name means 'Opred's farm'. The river Cray has its source here, and historically there were regular floods in the area. Although the railways arrived in 1868, modern Orpington is primarily a 20th-century town; however, there was some development in the 19th century along the High Street and at the north end of the village on the edge of Broomhill Common. After the railway station was enlarged in 1904, the developers moved in; development continued after World War I, when the High Street was transformed into a large shopping centre complete with cinemas. After World War II, the Ramsden council estate was built, and private housing was built to the south on the borders with Chelsfield and Farnborough. In the town centre, many early buildings were swept away when the Walnuts development was built to the east of the High Street in the 1970s. Orpington is today in the London Borough of Bromley.

▲ **ORPINGTON,** *The War Memorial and the High Street c1960* O107060

On the left is Maison Bartlett, a ladies' and gentlemen's hairdresser, and also the large frontage of Sherry's restaurant, with W E D Garvey on the right just behind the war memorial. Note the municipal flowerbeds around the memorial and down the centre of the main road. The Routemaster double-decker bus is advertising Aspro.

◄ **ORPINGTON,** *High Street c1955* O107017

The parade of shops behind the war memorial has survived later developments, but the occupants have changed and the distinctive diamond-shaped jeweller's clock has gone. The shops here include an estate agent's and Jay's fish shop. On the right, a road sweeper is cleaning the kerbs unimpeded by traffic. Also on the right are Priory Gardens.

ORPINGTON
The Commodore
c1950 O107046

The Commodore in the High Street was showing *The Underworld Story* starring Dan Duryea, a popular film star of the 1950s. Over the course of its life the cinema underwent many changes of identity. In1902 it was a Working Men's Club, in 1908 it became the Palace roller skating rink, and in 1911 Albert Spencer-May (landlord of The Old White Hart) opened a cinema on the site and called it the Carlton. In 1933 it became the Commodore. It eventually burned down, and the site today contains a branch of MacDonald's hamburger chain and a newsagent's.

ORPINGTON, *High Street c1960* O107059

The White Hart still stands on the High Street. Notice the off-licence sales attached to the main public house, a common feature at the time. It is selling Taylor Walker beers. Today it has had a face lift so as to appeal to a younger market. Some familiar High Street names can be seen, including Barclays Bank and K Shoes (on the right) and a Hovis sign.

PETTS WOOD

PETTS Wood has been rightly celebrated as the very model of a successful inter-war suburb. It reflects the vision of the developer Basil Scruby, who in the inter-war years set out to create the ideal garden suburb for middle-class commuters fourteen miles from London in rural Kent. To turn his dream into a reality, Scruby bought up 400 acres on either side of the London to Sevenoaks railway line, and started laying out his estate in 1927. To encourage potential buyers, he did a deal with Southern Railway under which he provided land and buildings and contributed to the construction of a railway station. Petts Wood station opened in 1928.

Building continued throughout the early 1930s on the eastern side of the railway; wide tree-lined streets and shopping centres were integrated with high-quality mock-Tudor housing. To finance his scheme, Scruby sold off land on the west of the railway line, where the resulting houses were plainer and more standardised than Scruby's original vision. Green belt regulations meant that there was little further development after 1945. Today Petts Wood is part of the London Borough of Bromley.

PETTS WOOD, *Station Square c1965* P377001

On Station Square, Petts Wood's original developer Basil Scruby had his agency offices, with a car ready to take prospective buyers to the show houses. There was still an estate office here in 1965 with neatly planted flower-beds in the foreground. The shops were grouped around a square, giving Petts Wood a logical centre and providing everything the affluent commuter needed in his home environment.

► **PETTS WOOD**
Fairway c1965
P377020

Down the road from
Station Square was
the Dunstonian
Garage, which sold
Hillman and Humber
cars and was built in
mock-Tudor style
under a canopy to
conform to the local
scheme. A Hillman
Humber Sunbeam
Singer is parked in the
road outside. The
National Petrol logo is
on the garage sign.

◄ **PETTS WOOD**
Queensway c1960
P377010

This was on the west side
of the railway line. The
typical mock-Tudor
parade of shops included
Tip Top Bakeries,
Summerfield's grocer's,
Queensway Fisheries (a
fish and chip shop), a
radio and TV shop, a
furniture shop and even a
wine merchant's,
denoting the middle-
class nature of the area.
Outside Cresswell's, on
the left, the shopkeeper is
sweeping the pavement.

▲ **PETTS WOOD,** *Frankswood Gardens Branch Library c1960* P377012

Another requirement for the successful middle-class suburb was a library. Here the branch library is built on the west side of the railway line. The road sign points to the public toilet.

◀**PETTS WOOD**
Willett Woods c1960 P377003

Willett Woods are situated north of the Petts Wood estate. The area was acquired by public subscription for the National Trust in 1927. In the centre is the Willett memorial sundial dedicated to William Willett of Chislehurst, a builder who was inspired to campaign for daylight saving when riding through Petts Wood in the early 1900s. On the south face it reads 'Horas non numero nisi æstivas' ('I will only tell the summer hours'). On the north face it reads: "This wood was purchased by public subscription as a tribute to the memory of William Willett the untiring advocate of 'summer time'. Erected 1927".

FARNBOROUGH

FARNBOROUGH first appears in an Anglo-Saxon charter of AD 862 as Fearn Biorg, 'the village in the ferns on the hill'. The local manor house was owned in the Middle Ages by Simon de Montfort. Until the by-pass was built in 1927, Farnborough lay directly on the A21, the old coach road to Hastings and the Kent coast. In the early 20th century, the village was popular with cyclists and Londoners on a day out. The surrounding countryside was used for market gardening, particularly strawberries, which flourished in the chalky soil. Farnborough today is in the London Borough of Bromley.

FARNBOROUGH, *The George and Dragon c1950* F185003

Today, the pub is known simply as The George; the original George and Dragon was a coaching inn at the junction of the High Street and Church Road. The original inn was demolished in 1936 and replaced by the typically thirties-style pub seen in the photograph. It was a popular destination for day trippers from London, and early photos show fleets of open-topped No 47 buses from Shoreditch pulled up outside. (There was usually a cockle and whelk stall outside to cater for the hungry East-Enders.) Judging by the 'No coaches' sign in the photo, in 1950 the pub was trying to attract a new clientele. Now a listed building, in 2003 The George was sold at auction and is closed pending redevelopment.

FARNBOROUGH, *Church Road c1955* F185012

The original coach road went along the High Street and Church Road, where several of the houses have the traditional Kentish clapboard fascias. In Church Road the path to the lych gate connects the village to the flint and brick church of St Giles the Abbot, which was rebuilt in the 17th century following storm damage. Wickens, one of the tearooms catering for the cyclists and day trippers, can be seen here.

▶ **FARNBOROUGH**
High Street c1955 F185006

▼ **FARNBOROUGH**
High Street c1965 F185025

The centre of the village is now a conservation area, with buildings dating back to the 17th century. Historically known as the Broadway, the High Street was (and is) the commercial heart of the village. The original school buildings (now listed) at the bottom of Start Hill Road (centre, F185006) are now in private hands, and the school has relocated to Farnborough Hill at the other end of the village. In the 1950s the village pond was filled in, and the allotments levelled. The Ladycroft and Elgal Close developments off the High Street were built in the 1960s and 1970s (F185025).

FARNBOROUGH, *High Street c1960* F185020

On the left of the photograph is The Change of Horses Inn, formerly known as The New Inn. After depositing its passengers for the night at The White Lion in Locksbottom (just north of Farnbrough), the stage continued into Farnborough, where the horse were turned out in the field opposite; the coachmen spent the night at The New Inn. The village Social Club can be seen on the right. Nearby, just out of view, is the historic Woodman pub. Two London transport Routemaster buses are parked in the middle distance near the junction with Church Road.

INDEX

Frith Book Co Titles

www.francisfrith.co.uk

The Frith Book Company publishes over 100 new titles each year. A selection of those currently available is listed below. For latest catalogue please contact Frith Book Co.

Town Books 96 pages, approximately 100 photos. **County and Themed Books** 128 pages, approximately 150 photos (unless specified). All titles hardback with laminated case and jacket, except those indicated pb (paperback).

Amersham, Chesham & Rickmansworth (pb)	1-85937-340-2	£9.99	Devon (pb)	1-85937-297-x	£9.99
Andover (pb)	1-85937-292-9	£9.99	Devon Churches (pb)	1-85937-250-3	£9.99
Aylesbury (pb)	1-85937-227-9	£9.99	Dorchester (pb)	1-85937-307-0	£9.99
Barnstaple (pb)	1-85937-300-3	£9.99	Dorset (pb)	1-85937-269-4	£9.99
Basildon Living Memories (pb)	1-85937-515-4	£9.99	Dorset Coast (pb)	1-85937-299-6	£9.99
Bath (pb)	1-85937-419-0	£9.99	Dorset Living Memories (pb)	1-85937-584-7	£9.99
Bedford (pb)	1-85937-205-8	£9.99	Down the Severn (pb)	1-85937-560-x	£9.99
Bedfordshire Living Memories	1-85937-513-8	£14.99	Down The Thames (pb)	1-85937-278-3	£9.99
Belfast (pb)	1-85937-303-8	£9.99	Down the Trent	1-85937-311-9	£14.99
Berkshire (pb)	1-85937-191-4	£9.99	East Anglia (pb)	1-85937-265-1	£9.99
Berkshire Churches	1-85937-170-1	£17.99	East Grinstead (pb)	1-85937-138-8	£9.99
Berkshire Living Memories	1-85937-332-1	£14.99	East London	1-85937-080-2	£14.99
Black Country	1-85937-497-2	£12.99	East Sussex (pb)	1-85937-606-1	£9.99
Blackpool (pb)	1-85937-393-3	£9.99	Eastbourne (pb)	1-85937-399-2	£9.99
Bognor Regis (pb)	1-85937-431-x	£9.99	Edinburgh (pb)	1-85937-193-0	£8.99
Bournemouth (pb)	1-85937-545-6	£9.99	England In The 1880s	1-85937-331-3	£17.99
Bradford (pb)	1-85937-204-x	£9.99	Essex - Second Selection	1-85937-456-5	£14.99
Bridgend (pb)	1-85937-386-0	£7.99	Essex (pb)	1-85937-270-8	£9.99
Bridgwater (pb)	1-85937-305-4	£9.99	Essex Coast	1-85937-342-9	£14.99
Bridport (pb)	1-85937-327-5	£9.99	Essex Living Memories	1-85937-490-5	£14.99
Brighton (pb)	1-85937-192-2	£8.99	Exeter	1-85937-539-1	£9.99
Bristol (pb)	1-85937-264-3	£9.99	Exmoor (pb)	1-85937-608-8	£9.99
British Life A Century Ago (pb)	1-85937-213-9	£9.99	Falmouth (pb)	1-85937-594-4	£9.99
Buckinghamshire (pb)	1-85937-200-7	£9.99	Folkestone (pb)	1-85937-124-8	£9.99
Camberley (pb)	1-85937-222-8	£9.99	Frome (pb)	1-85937-317-8	£9.99
Cambridge (pb)	1-85937-422-0	£9.99	Glamorgan	1-85937-488-3	£14.99
Cambridgeshire (pb)	1-85937-420-4	£9.99	Glasgow (pb)	1-85937-190-6	£9.99
Cambridgeshire Villages	1-85937-523-5	£14.99	Glastonbury (pb)	1-85937-338-0	£7.99
Canals And Waterways (pb)	1-85937-291-0	£9.99	Gloucester (pb)	1-85937-232-5	£9.99
Canterbury Cathedral (pb)	1-85937-179-5	£9.99	Gloucestershire (pb)	1-85937-561-8	£9.99
Cardiff (pb)	1-85937-093-4	£9.99	Great Yarmouth (pb)	1-85937-426-3	£9.99
Carmarthenshire (pb)	1-85937-604-5	£9.99	Greater Manchester (pb)	1-85937-266-x	£9.99
Chelmsford (pb)	1-85937-310-0	£9.99	Guildford (pb)	1-85937-410-7	£9.99
Cheltenham (pb)	1-85937-095-0	£9.99	Hampshire (pb)	1-85937-279-1	£9.99
Cheshire (pb)	1-85937-271-6	£9.99	Harrogate (pb)	1-85937-423-9	£9.99
Chester (pb)	1-85937-382 8	£9.99	Hastings and Bexhill (pb)	1-85937-131-0	£9.99
Chesterfield (pb)	1-85937-378-x	£9.99	Heart of Lancashire (pb)	1-85937-197-3	£9.99
Chichester (pb)	1-85937-228-7	£9.99	Helston (pb)	1-85937-214-7	£9.99
Churches of East Cornwall (pb)	1-85937-249-x	£9.99	Hereford (pb)	1-85937-175-2	£9.99
Churches of Hampshire (pb)	1-85937-207-4	£9.99	Herefordshire (pb)	1-85937-567-7	£9.99
Cinque Ports & Two Ancient Towns	1-85937-492-1	£14.99	Herefordshire Living Memories	1-85937-514-6	£14.99
Colchester (pb)	1-85937-188-4	£8.99	Hertfordshire (pb)	1-85937-247-3	£9.99
Cornwall (pb)	1-85937-229-5	£9.99	Horsham (pb)	1-85937-432-8	£9.99
Cornwall Living Memories	1-85937-248-1	£14.99	Humberside (pb)	1-85937-605-3	£9.99
Cotswolds (pb)	1-85937-230-9	£9.99	Hythe, Romney Marsh, Ashford (pb)	1-85937-256-2	£9.99
Cotswolds Living Memories	1-85937-255-4	£14.99	Ipswich (pb)	1-85937-424-7	£9.99
County Durham (pb)	1-85937-398-4	£9.99	Isle of Man (pb)	1-85937-268-6	£9.99
Croydon Living Memories (pb)	1-85937-162-0	£9.99	Isle of Wight (pb)	1-85937-429-8	£9.99
Cumbria (pb)	1-85937-621-5	£9.99	Isle of Wight Living Memories	1-85937-304-6	£14.99
Derby (pb)	1-85937-367-4	£9.99	Kent (pb)	1-85937-189-2	£9.99
Derbyshire (pb)	1-85937-196-5	£9.99	Kent Living Memories(pb)	1-85937-401-8	£9.99
Derbyshire Living Memories	1-85937-330-5	£14.99	Kings Lynn (pb)	1-85937-334-8	£9.99

Available from your local bookshop or from the publisher

Frith Book Co Titles (continued)

Title	ISBN	Price	Title	ISBN	Price
Lake District (pb)	1-85937-275-9	£9.99	Sherborne (pb)	1-85937-301-1	£9.99
Lancashire Living Memories	1-85937-335-6	£14.99	Shrewsbury (pb)	1-85937-325-9	£9.99
Lancaster, Morecambe, Heysham (pb)	1-85937-233-3	£9.99	Shropshire (pb)	1-85937-326-7	£9.99
Leeds (pb)	1-85937-202-3	£9.99	Shropshire Living Memories	1-85937-643-6	£14.99
Leicester (pb)	1-85937-381-x	£9.99	Somerset	1-85937-153-1	£14.99
Leicestershire & Rutland Living Memories	1-85937-500-6	£12.99	South Devon Coast	1-85937-107-8	£14.99
Leicestershire (pb)	1-85937-185-x	£9.99	South Devon Living Memories (pb)	1-85937-609-6	£9.99
Lighthouses	1-85937-257-0	£9.99	South East London (pb)	1-85937-263-5	£9.99
Lincoln (pb)	1-85937-380-1	£9.99	South Somerset	1-85937-318-6	£14.99
Lincolnshire (pb)	1-85937-433-6	£9.99	South Wales	1-85937-519-7	£14.99
Liverpool and Merseyside (pb)	1-85937-234-1	£9.99	Southampton (pb)	1-85937-427-1	£9.99
London (pb)	1-85937-183-3	£9.99	Southend (pb)	1-85937-313-5	£9.99
London Living Memories	1-85937-454-9	£14.99	Southport (pb)	1-85937-425-5	£9.99
Ludlow (pb)	1-85937-176-0	£9.99	St Albans (pb)	1-85937-341-0	£9.99
Luton (pb)	1-85937-235-x	£9.99	St Ives (pb)	1-85937-415-8	£9.99
Maidenhead (pb)	1-85937-339-9	£9.99	Stafford Living Memories (pb)	1-85937-503-0	£9.99
Maidstone (pb)	1-85937-391-7	£9.99	Staffordshire (pb)	1-85937-308-9	£9.99
Manchester (pb)	1-85937-198-1	£9.99	Stourbridge (pb)	1-85937-530-8	£9.99
Marlborough (pb)	1-85937-336-4	£9.99	Stratford upon Avon (pb)	1-85937-388-7	£9.99
Middlesex	1-85937-158-2	£14.99	Suffolk (pb)	1-85937-221-x	£9.99
Monmouthshire	1-85937-532-4	£14.99	Suffolk Coast (pb)	1-85937-610-x	£9.99
New Forest (pb)	1-85937-390-9	£9.99	Surrey (pb)	1-85937-240-6	£9.99
Newark (pb)	1-85937-366-6	£9.99	Surrey Living Memories	1-85937-328-3	£14.99
Newport, Wales (pb)	1-85937-258-9	£9.99	Sussex (pb)	1-85937-184-1	£9.99
Newquay (pb)	1-85937-421-2	£9.99	Sutton (pb)	1-85937-337-2	£9.99
Norfolk (pb)	1-85937-195-7	£9.99	Swansea (pb)	1-85937-167-1	£9.99
Norfolk Broads	1-85937-486-7	£14.99	Taunton (pb)	1-85937-314-3	£9.99
Norfolk Living Memories (pb)	1-85937-402-6	£9.99	Tees Valley & Cleveland (pb)	1-85937-623-1	£9.99
North Buckinghamshire	1-85937-626-6	£14.99	Teignmouth (pb)	1-85937-370-4	£7.99
North Devon Living Memories	1-85937-261-9	£14.99	Thanet (pb)	1-85937-116-7	£9.99
North Hertfordshire	1-85937-547-2	£14.99	Tiverton (pb)	1-85937-178-7	£9.99
North London (pb)	1-85937-403-4	£9.99	Torbay (pb)	1-85937-597-9	£9.99
North Somerset	1-85937-302-x	£14.99	Truro (pb)	1-85937-598-7	£9.99
North Wales (pb)	1-85937-298-8	£9.99	Victorian & Edwardian Dorset	1-85937-254-6	£14.99
North Yorkshire (pb)	1-85937-236-8	£9.99	Victorian & Edwardian Kent (pb)	1-85937-624-X	£9.99
Northamptonshire Living Memories	1-85937-529-4	£14.99	Victorian & Edwardian Maritime Album (pb)	1-85937-622-3	£9.99
Northamptonshire	1-85937-150-7	£14.99	Victorian and Edwardian Sussex (pb)	1-85937-625-8	£9.99
Northumberland Tyne & Wear (pb)	1-85937-281-3	£9.99	Villages of Devon (pb)	1-85937-293-7	£9.99
Northumberland	1-85937-522-7	£14.99	Villages of Kent (pb)	1-85937-294-5	£9.99
Norwich (pb)	1-85937-194-9	£8.99	Villages of Sussex (pb)	1-85937-295-3	£9.99
Nottingham (pb)	1-85937-324-0	£9.99	Warrington (pb)	1-85937-507-3	£9.99
Nottinghamshire (pb)	1-85937-187-6	£9.99	Warwick (pb)	1-85937-518-9	£9.99
Oxford (pb)	1-85937-411-5	£9.99	Warwickshire (pb)	1-85937-203-1	£9.99
Oxfordshire (pb)	1-85937-430-1	£9.99	Welsh Castles (pb)	1-85937-322-4	£9.99
Oxfordshire Living Memories	1-85937-525-1	£14.99	West Midlands (pb)	1-85937-289-9	£9.99
Paignton (pb)	1-85937-374-7	£7.99	West Sussex (pb)	1-85937-607-x	£9.99
Peak District (pb)	1-85937-280-5	£9.99	West Yorkshire (pb)	1-85937-201-5	£9.99
Pembrokeshire	1-85937-262-7	£14.99	Weston Super Mare (pb)	1-85937-306-2	£9.99
Penzance (pb)	1-85937-595-2	£9.99	Weymouth (pb)	1-85937-209-0	£9.99
Peterborough (pb)	1-85937-219-8	£9.99	Wiltshire (pb)	1-85937-277-5	£9.99
Picturesque Harbours	1-85937-208-2	£14.99	Wiltshire Churches (pb)	1-85937-171-x	£9.99
Piers	1-85937-237-6	£17.99	Wiltshire Living Memories (pb)	1-85937-396-8	£9.99
Plymouth (pb)	1-85937-389-5	£9.99	Winchester (pb)	1-85937-428-x	£9.99
Poole & Sandbanks (pb)	1-85937-251-1	£9.99	Windsor (pb)	1-85937-333-x	£9.99
Preston (pb)	1-85937-212-0	£9.99	Wokingham & Bracknell (pb)	1-85937-329-1	£9.99
Reading (pb)	1-85937-238-4	£9.99	Woodbridge (pb)	1-85937-498-0	£9.99
Redhill to Reigate (pb)	1-85937-596-0	£9.99	Worcester (pb)	1-85937-165-5	£9.99
Ringwood (pb)	1-85937-384-4	£7.99	Worcestershire Living Memories	1-85937-489-1	£14.99
Romford (pb)	1-85937-319-4	£9.99	Worcestershire	1-85937-152-3	£14.99
Royal Tunbridge Wells (pb)	1-85937-504-9	£9.99	York (pb)	1-85937-199-x	£9.99
Salisbury (pb)	1-85937-239-2	£9.99	Yorkshire (pb)	1-85937-186-8	£9.99
Scarborough (pb)	1-85937-379-8	£9.99	Yorkshire Coastal Memories	1-85937-506-5	£14.99
Sevenoaks and Tonbridge (pb)	1-85937-392-5	£9.99	Yorkshire Dales	1-85937-502-2	£14.99
Sheffield & South Yorks (pb)	1-85937-267-8	£9.99	Yorkshire Living Memories (pb)	1-85937-397-6	£9.99

See Frith books on the internet at www.francisfrith.co.uk

FRITH PRODUCTS & SERVICES

Francis Frith would doubtless be pleased to know that the pioneering publishing venture he started in 1860 still continues today. Over a hundred and forty years later, The Francis Frith Collection continues in the same innovative tradition and is now one of the foremost publishers of vintage photographs in the world. Some of the current activities include:

Interior Decoration

Today Frith's photographs can be seen framed and as giant wall murals in thousands of pubs, restaurants, hotels, banks, retail stores and other public buildings throughout the country. In every case they enhance the unique local atmosphere of the places they depict and provide reminders of gentler days in an increasingly busy and frenetic world.

Product Promotions

Frith products are used by many major companies to promote the sales of their own products or to reinforce their own history and heritage. Frith promotions have been used by Hovis bread, Courage beers, Scots Porage Oats, Colman's mustard, Cadbury's foods, Mellow Birds coffee, Dunhill pipe tobacco, Guinness, and Bulmer's Cider.

Genealogy and Family History

As the interest in family history and roots grows world-wide, more and more people are turning to Frith's photographs of Great Britain for images of the towns, villages and streets where their ancestors lived; and, of course, photographs of the churches and chapels where their ancestors were christened, married and buried are an essential part of every genealogy tree and family album.

Frith Products

All Frith photographs are available Framed or just as Mounted Prints and Posters (size 23 x 16 inches). These may be ordered from the address below. From time to time other products - Address Books, Calendars, Table Mats, etc - are available.

The Internet

Already fifty thousand Frith photographs can be viewed and purchased on the internet through the Frith websites and a myriad of partner sites.

For more detailed information on Frith companies and products, look at these sites:

www.francisfrith.co.uk
www.francisfrith.com
(for North American visitors)

See the complete list of Frith Books at:

www.francisfrith.co.uk

This web site is regularly updated with the latest list of publications from the Frith Book Company. If you wish to buy books relating to another part of the country that your local bookshop does not stock, you may purchase on-line.

For further information, trade, or author enquiries please contact us at the address below:
The Francis Frith Collection, Frith's Barn, Teffont, Salisbury, Wiltshire, England SP3 5QP.
Tel: +44 (0)1722 716 376 Fax: +44 (0)1722 716 881 Email: sales@francisfrith.co.uk

See Frith books on the internet at www.francisfrith.co.uk

FREE MOUNTED PRINT

Mounted Print
Overall size 14 x 11 inches

Fill in and cut out this voucher and return
it with your remittance for £2.25 (to cover postage and handling). Offer valid for delivery to UK addresses only.

Choose any photograph included in this book.
Your SEPIA print will be A4 in size. It will be mounted in a cream mount with a burgundy rule line (overall size 14 x 11 inches).

**Order additional Mounted Prints
at HALF PRICE (only £7.49 each*)**
If you would like to order more Frith prints from this book, possibly as gifts for friends and family, you can buy them at half price (with no additional postage and handling costs).

Have your Mounted Prints framed
For an extra £14.95 per print* you can have your mounted print(s) framed in an elegant polished wood and gilt moulding, overall size 16 x 13 inches (no additional postage and handling required).

---

* IMPORTANT!

These special prices are only available if you order at the same time as you order your free mounted print. You must use the ORIGINAL VOUCHER on this page (no copies permitted). We can only despatch to one address.

Send completed Voucher form to:
The Francis Frith Collection, Frith's Barn, Teffont, Salisbury, Wiltshire SP3 5QP

Voucher for *FREE* and Reduced Price Frith Prints

Please do not photocopy this voucher. Only the original is valid, so please fill it in, cut it out and return it to us with your order.

Picture ref no	Page no	Qty	Mounted @ £7.49	Framed + £14.95	Total Cost
		1	Free of charge*	£	£
			£7.49	£	£
			£7.49	£	£
			£7.49	£	£
			£7.49	£	£
			£7.49	£	£
Please allow 28 days for delivery			* Post & handling (UK)		£2.25
			Total Order Cost		£

Title of this book . . . .

I enclose a cheque/postal order for £ . . . .
made payable to 'The Francis Frith Collection'

OR please debit my Mastercard / Visa / Switch / Amex card
(credit cards please on all overseas orders), details below

Card Number

Issue No (Switch only)   Valid from (Amex/Switch)

Expires   Signature

Name Mr/Mrs/Ms ....

Address ....

....

....

.... Postcode ....

Daytime Tel No ....

Email ....

Valid to 31/12/05

Free Print – see overleaf

Would you like to find out more about Francis Frith?

We have recently recruited some entertaining speakers who are happy to visit local groups, clubs and societies to give an illustrated talk documenting Frith's travels and photographs. If you are a member of such a group and are interested in hosting a presentation, we would love to hear from you.

Our speakers bring with them a small selection of our local town and county books, together with sample prints. They are happy to take orders. A small proportion of the order value is donated to the group who have hosted the presentation. The talks are therefore an excellent way of fundraising for small groups and societies.

Can you help us with information about any of the Frith photographs in this book?

We are gradually compiling an historical record for each of the photographs in the Frith archive. It is always fascinating to find out the names of the people shown in the pictures, as well as insights into the shops, buildings and other features depicted.

If you recognize anyone in the photographs in this book, or if you have information not already included in the author's caption, do let us know. We would love to hear from you, and will try to publish it in future books or articles.

Our production team

Frith books are produced by a small dedicated team at offices in the converted Grade II listed 18th-century barn at Teffont near Salisbury, illustrated above. Most have worked with the Frith Collection for many years. All have in common one quality: they have a passion for the Frith Collection. The team is constantly expanding, but currently includes:

Jason Buck, John Buck, Douglas Mitchell-Burns, Ruth Butler, Heather Crisp, Isobel Hall, Julian Hight, Peter Horne, James Kinnear, Karen Kinnear, Tina Leary, David Marsh, Sue Molloy, Kate Rotondetto, Dean Scource, Eliza Sackett, Terence Sackett, Sandra Sampson, Adrian Sanders, Sandra Sanger, Julia Skinner, Lewis Taylor, Shelley Tolcher and Lorraine Tuck.

BOOK BARN BOOKS

3525114-6

 £6.00